True Survival

JULIANE KOEPCKE

LOST
IN PERU

Virginia Loh-Hagan

45th Parallel Press

Published in the United States of America by Cherry Lake Publishing
Ann Arbor, Michigan
www.cherrylakepublishing.com

Reading Adviser: Marla Conn MS, Ed., Literacy specialist, Read-Ability, Inc.
Book Designer: Felicia Macheske

45th Parallel Press is an imprint of Cherry Lake Publishing.

Library of Congress Cataloging-in-Publication Data

Names: Loh-Hagan, Virginia, author.
Title: Juliane Koepcke : lost in Peru / by Virginia Loh-Hagan.
Other titles: Lost in Peru
Description: Ann Arbor : Cherry Lake Publishing, [2018] | Series: True survival | Includes bibliographical references and index.
Identifiers: LCCN 2017030502| ISBN 9781534107700 (hardcover) | ISBN 9781534108691 (pbk.) | ISBN 9781534109681 (PDF) | ISBN 9781534120679 (hosted ebook)
Subjects: LCSH: Airplane crash survival—Peru—Juvenile literature. | Aircraft accidents—Peru—Juvenile literature. | Koepcke, Juliane—Juvenile literature.
Classification: LCC TL553.9 .L64 2018 | DDC 363.12/4092 [B] —dc23
LC record available at https://lccn.loc.gov/2017030502

Cherry Lake Publishing would like to acknowledge the work of The Partnership for 21st Century Skills. Please visit *www.p21.org* for more information.

Printed in the United States of America
Corporate Graphics

table of contents

chapter one

Leaving on a Jet Plane

Who is Juliane Koepcke? What was LANSA Flight 508?

Juliane Koepcke was born in 1954. She's German. But she was born in Lima. Lima is in Peru. She moved to the Amazon rainforest in Peru at age 14. Her parents set up a research station there. She wanted to be like her parents. They were **scientists**. Some scientists study the natural world.

She stayed with them for 2 years. She became a "jungle child." Then she moved back to Lima. Her mother went with her. Koepcke **graduated** from high school. Graduate means to finish school. She wanted to stay for her celebration. Her mother wanted to fly back to the rainforest. Her father was there. They wanted to be together as a family.

The Koepckes studied animals. They were experts in birds.

spotlight biography

Hans-Wilhelm Koepcke was Juliane Koepcke's father. He was a famous animal scientist. He mainly studied birds and reptiles. He wrote a famous book about life-forms. He was born in 1914. He was born in Germany. He got a doctorate in natural sciences. He moved to a rainforest in Peru. He and his wife, Maria, studied wildlife there. They founded a research station. They called it Panguana. Panguana is a native bird. The station was built on stilts. The area was a "hotspot of biodiversity." This means they were able to study a lot of different things. We know a lot about this area because of the Koepckes. The rest of the Amazon rainforest is still a mystery. After the crash, he was very sad. He left Peru. He moved back to Germany. He died in 2000.

Koepcke begged her mother. She wanted to stay a little longer. Her mother agreed. They would take a late flight. They would fly on Christmas Eve.

The airport was packed. They were on LANSA Flight 508. Their flight was 7 hours late. Koepcke and her mother finally got on the plane. Koepcke's father was going to meet them.

There were 86 **passengers** on the plane. Passengers are people who fly on planes. There were 6 members of the **crew**. Crew means workers. That was a total of 92 people.

Everything was fine for the first 25 minutes.

Airports can be very crowded around holidays.

chapter two

Struck by Lightning

What happened to Koepcke's flight?
What happened to Koepcke?

There was a bad storm. The plane bounced up and down. Things fell. Things were thrown around. People cried. People screamed.

Koepcke held her mother's hand. Koepcke's mother said, "That is the end. It's all over." Those were the last words Koepcke heard from her.

Lightning hit the plane. The gas tank blew up. The wings fell off. The plane broke. It broke in the air. It crashed in a rainforest in Peru.

The plane fell 10,000 feet (3,048 meters). Koepcke was strapped in her seat. She flipped head over heels. She passed out. She crashed through the **canopy**. The canopy is the treetops. She landed on the ground.

The plane was 21,000 feet (6,401 m) in the air when lightning struck.

She woke up the next day. Her collarbone was broken. Her right arm had a cut. Her right eye was swollen shut. Her knee was torn. Her legs had deep cuts.

She thinks the seat saved her life. She said, "It must have turned and **buffered** the crash." Buffered means to protect against. The seat was like a shield. It gave her padding. The seats on the side of her helped, too. They served as a **parachute**. Parachutes are like umbrellas. This slowed her fall. The storm winds and leafy trees gave her a soft landing.

The flight was supposed to be less than an hour long.

explained by science

Scientists crashed a plane. They did it on purpose. They did this on April 27, 2012. They did it in Mexico. They wanted to study plane crashes. They put cameras on the plane. They put crash test dummies in it. Crash test dummies are life-size models of people. Scientists crashed the plane into the ground. They filmed it. It fell at a rate of 1,500 feet (457 m) per minute. The plane hit at 140 miles (225 kilometers) per hour. It broke into several parts. They found out several things. Passengers at the front are the most at risk. Passengers seated by the wings would have injuries. But they were likely to survive. Passengers at the back were the safest. Seatbelts saved people's lives. So does bracing for impact. This means hunching over toward the seat in front of you.

Koepcke shouted for her mother. She looked for her. She couldn't find her. Her mother had been sitting next to her. She was gone.

Koepcke looked for others. She didn't find anyone near her. She was alone. The crash happened on December 24, 1971. Koepcke was the only survivor. She was 17 years old.

After the crash, Koepcke heard planes. She couldn't see them. The planes couldn't see her. The trees were too thick. She had to get into an open area. She needed to get saved.

◄ It's hard to get rescued in the rainforest. The canopy is thick.

chapter three

Jungle Life

How did Koepcke know how to survive? What were her challenges? How did she live?

Koepcke had lived in the jungle. So she had some survival skills. But she was still unprepared.

She had worn a short dress without sleeves. She had no protection from the sun. She had fair skin. The sun in Peru is harsh. She got sunburned.

She lost her glasses. She's **nearsighted**. She can only see what's in front of her face. She had worn white shoes. But one shoe was lost. She used the shoe. She tested the ground ahead of her. She walked through the thick jungle.

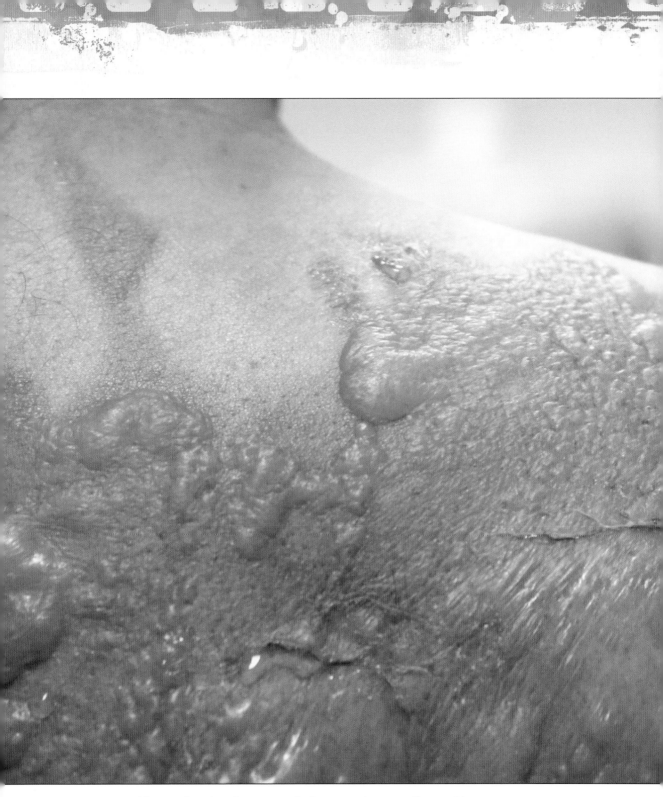

Koepcke had second-degree burns from the sun.

She found a small stream. She walked in the water. The water came to her knees. She walked downstream. That's where people would be. The stream gave her clean water. It gave her a path through the rainforest. This way she could avoid poisonous plants.

But there were other dangers. There were **piranhas**. Piranhas are dangerous fish. They have teeth. They eat meat. They live in shallow water. So Koepcke walked in the middle. She saw caimans. Caimans are like alligators. But she knew caimans rarely attacked humans.

Waterways are the highways of the Amazon rainforest.

would you?

- **Would you visit the Amazon rainforest?** This rainforest is over 1 billion acres (405 million hectares). It has thick forests. It has a lot of rainfall. It has many dangerous animals. It has many poisonous plants. It's also beautiful. It has many different life-forms.

- **Would you swim in a river with caimans?** They have many sharp teeth. They have powerful jaws. They have scaly skin. They're dangerous hunters. But they rarely attack humans. They prefer smaller prey. They like prey they can swallow in one bite.

- **Would you eat a plant you didn't know?** Each year, there are 10 to 60 deaths caused by plant poisoning. Amazon rainforests have a lot of poisonous plants. Some plants are more dangerous than snakes.

She worried about snakes. She worried about bugs. She couldn't sleep at night. Bugs bit her. Her bites got infected. She thought she'd lose her arm. Her arm was being eaten alive.

Koepcke had a bag of candy. She had found it at the crash site. That was her only food. It lasted four days. It was the rainy season. So, there was no fruit. She didn't have a knife. So she couldn't cut back plants. She couldn't hunt. She couldn't catch fish. She didn't have fire. She couldn't cook. She didn't eat anything she didn't know. She was scared of being poisoned.

◄ Bullet ants have the most painful sting of any insect. They are found in the rainforest.

chapter four

The Girl in the Crash

How did she get rescued? What happened to her mother?

She was lonely. She was always in danger. She saw **wreckage**. Wreckage is crash remains. She saw **corpses**. Corpses are dead bodies. She kept looking for her mother. She never found her.

She was sad. She was tired. She was hungry. She needed doctors. She couldn't stand up straight.

She walked for 10 days. She finally found a boat. She found a hut. The hut had the boat's motor and gas. She poured gas on her cuts. **Maggots** came out of her cuts. Maggots are fly larva. They eat flesh. Koepcke counted more than 30 maggots.

Finding a boat meant there were people nearby.

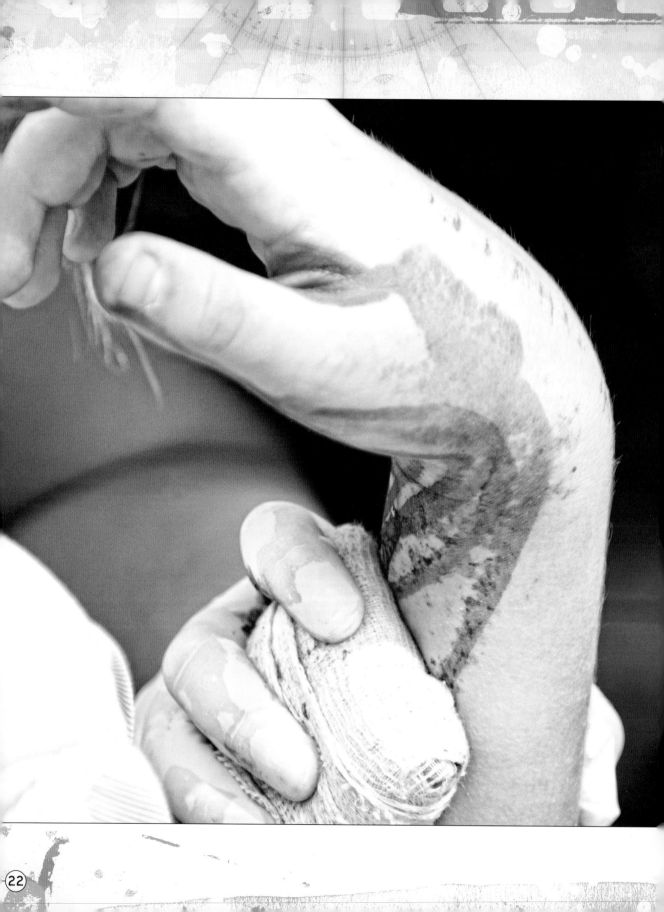

She waited to be saved. She spent the night there.

The next day, she heard voices. Help came. Lumber workers came to use the boat. **Lumber** is the business of cutting wood. The workers found Koepcke. They were confused.

Koepcke talked to them in Spanish. She said, "I'm a girl who was in the LANSA crash. My name is Juliane."

The workers helped her. They fixed her cuts. They fed her.

◄ The lumber workers treated Koepcke's injuries.

People were stunned that Koepcke survived.

They took her down the river. There was a town there. This boat trip took 7 hours. They went to a lumber station.

A **pilot** helped. Pilots fly planes. She was flown to a hospital. Her father was waiting for her. He could barely talk. Koepcke and her father hugged. They held each other for a long time.

On January 12, her mother's body was found. Her mother had survived the crash. But she died soon after. She died from **injuries**. Injuries are when harm is done to the body. Her mother couldn't move. She was stuck.

survival tips

LOST IN A JUNGLE!

- Find running water. Follow it. It will lead to bigger water sources. That's where you'll find help. Also, this will help you not get lost.

- Pick your feet up from the ground. Avoid tripping over roots.

- Cover your skin. Avoid bug bites. Avoid sunburns.

- Wear rubber shoes. If you don't have any, wrap your feet in plastic bags. Wear shoes on top of the plastic bags.

- Save your energy. Walk slowly.

- Get a long branch. Use it as a walking stick. Use it to move things out of the way.

- Take shelter on the highest ground possible.

- Don't store food. This will attract animals. The food will also rot because of the heat.

chapter five

Saving Rainforests

What happened after Koepcke was rescued? What is she doing in Peru?

Koepcke returned to Lima. She healed. She went to school. She got too famous. People wanted to hear about her survival story. **Journalists** followed her around. Journalists are people who write news stories. Her father sent her to Germany.

Koepcke went to the university. She got a **doctorate**. Doctorates are the highest degrees people can earn. She studied **mammals**. Mammals are warm-blooded animals. They give live birth. Koepcke became an expert in bats. She married Erich Diller. Diller is an expert on wasps.

Koepcke said she has bad dreams. She's still sad about all the deaths. She feels guilty about being the only survivor.

People who study mammals are called mammalogists.

Rest in Peace

Maria Koepcke was Koepcke's mother. She was a famous bird scientist. She was born and raised in Germany. She had a doctorate. She went to Kiel University. She moved to Peru. She married Hans-Wilhelm Koepcke. They married in 1950. They worked together. They studied wildlife in Peru. Most bird scientists were men. Some people were unfair to Maria because she was a woman. That didn't stop her. She became successful. Three species of birds were named after her. She was in the crash with Koepcke. She landed in a different area. She was badly hurt. She died. She instilled a love of animals and science in her daughter. She'll be remembered as a mom and a scientist.

She still goes to Peru. She goes there twice a year. She said, "Long flights are difficult."

She goes to her parents' research station. She's turning it into a nature **reserve**. A reserve is like a park or zoo. This is a special place. It protects animals and plants.

Koepcke made it bigger. She added more land. She said, "I'm now trying to save the rainforest that saved my life." She welcomes scientists from all over the world. She wants people to study the rainforests. She wants people to protect it.

Koepcke wrote a book about her story.

Did You Know?

- Over half of Peru is covered by jungle and rainforests.

- Peru's rainforests are called the "world's lungs." More than 20 percent of Earth's oxygen is made in this area.

- Koepcke's first pet was a parrot. The parrot's name was Tobias. Her parents had him before Koepcke was born. Tobias was jealous of Koepcke.

- Koepcke learned a lot from her father. Their dog had maggots. He poured gas on the dog. She remembered this.

- Koepcke saw a king vulture. Vultures are big birds. She saw it on the fourth day. She was scared. Vultures only land on dead bodies. She knew corpses from the crash were nearby.

- The lumber workers thought Koepcke was a water goddess. They thought she was half-dolphin and half-woman.

- Koepcke's mother didn't like flying. She thought it was unnatural for non-birds to fly.

- The plane's parts fell over a 5.8-square-mile (15 sq km) area. It was the biggest search in Peru's history. The forests are thick. It's hard to see.

- Peru has a lot of vampire bats. When Koepcke was a child, a bat bit her big toe. She was sleeping.

Consider This!

Take a Position: Some believe Koepcke's survival was a miracle. They're surprised she lived. They think she was lucky. Do you think that's true? Was she lucky? Or was she skilled? Or both? Argue your point with reasons and evidence.

Say What? There are different types of scientists. Biologists are a type of scientist. They study life-forms. There are different types of biologists. Koepcke is a mammalogist. She studies mammals. Her parents were ornithologists. They studied birds. Research a type of scientist. Explain what these scientists do.

Think About It! Koepcke is scared of flying. She said, "I have, since that time, lost my trust in planes and pilots. I listen to every sound and am nervous every time I fly." Scientists say more people die in car accidents than plane accidents. Why are people afraid to fly? Are you afraid to fly?

Learn More

- Koepcke, Juliane, and Ross Benjamin, trans. *When I Fell from the Sky*. Green Bay, WI: TitleTown Publishing, 2011.

- Kyi, Tanya Lloyd, and David Parkins, illust. *When the Worst Happens: Extraordinary Stories of Survival*. Toronto: Annick Press, 2014.

- Spalding, Frank. *Plane Crash: True Stories of Survival*. New York: Rosen, 2007.

- Surges, Carol S. *The Science of a Plane Crash*. Ann Arbor, MI: Cherry Lake Publishing, 2015.

Glossary

buffered (BUHF-urd) protected against

canopy (KAN-uh-pee) top layer of the rainforest, the treetops

corpses (KORPS-iz) dead bodies

crew (KROO) workers, people who work for the airlines

doctorate (DAHK-tur-uht) the highest degree earned from a university

graduated (GRAJ-oo-ate-id) finished school

injuries (IN-jur-eez) harm done to the body

journalists (JUR-nuh-lists) people who write news stories

lumber (LUHM-bur) business of cutting wood

maggots (MAG-uhts) the larvae of flies, the worm stage of a fly's life cycle

mammals (MAM-uhlz) animals that are warm-blooded, that give live birth, and that feed their young milk

nearsighted (NEER-sye-tid) only able to see what is in front of their faces

parachute (PAH-ruh-shoot) a device that looks like the top of an umbrella that fills with air and slows down a fall

passengers (PAS-uhn-jurz) people who are flying on a plane as customers

pilot (PYE-luht) a person who flies planes

piranhas (puh-RAH-nuhz) fish with teeth that eat flesh

reserve (rih-ZURV) a protected area like a park or zoo

scientists (SYE-uhn-tists) people who study science

wreckage (REK-ij) remains of a crash

Index

About the Author

Dr. Virginia Loh-Hagan is an author, university professor, former classroom teacher, and curriculum designer. She went to Belize. That's the closest she's been to Peru. She lives in San Diego with her very tall husband and very naughty dogs. To learn more about her, visit www.virginialoh.com.